Animal Detectives
Search for the Facts

WHALES AND DOLPHINS

Anne O'Daly

Raintree is an imprint of Capstone Global Library Limited, a company incorporated in England and Wales having its registered office at 264 Banbury Road, Oxford, OX2 7DY – Registered company number: 6695582

www.raintree.co.uk
myorders@raintree.co.uk

© Brown Bear Books Limited 2021
Ths edition published by Raintree in 2021

All rights reserved. No part of this publication may be reproduced in any form or by any means (including photocopying or storing it in any medium by electronic means and whether or not transiently or incidentally to some other use of this publication) without the written permission of the copyright owner, except in accordance with the provisions of the Copyright, Designs and Patents Act 1988 or under the terms of a licence issued by the Copyright Licensing Agency, Saffron House, 6–10 Kirby Street, London EC1N 8TS (www.cla.co.uk). Applications for the copyright owner's written permission should be addressed to the publisher.

Created by Brown Bear Books Ltd
Design Manager: Keith Davis
Children's Publisher: Anne O'Daly
Picture Manager: Sophie Mortimer
Printed and bound in India

ISBN 978 1 4747 9849 5 (hardback)
ISBN 978 1 4747 9855 6 (paperback)

British Library Cataloguing in Publication Data
A full catalogue record for this book is available from the British Library.

London Borough of Enfield	
91200000717316	
Askews & Holts	02-Apr-2021
J599.5 JUNIOR NON-FI	
ENBUSH	

Picture Credits
Cover: Shutterstock: Tomas Kotouc; Interior: iStock: avs_it 4bl, George Clerk 18, Jen DeVos 6, eco2drew 4-5b, Foto4440 14, Janos 4l, John Mccormack Photo 5tl, pvcrossi 16, Mogens Trolle 5tr; NOAA Photo Library: Dr Krisin Laidre, Polar Science Center 5r, 20; Shutterstock: rm 5br, Triduza Studio 16-17, 18-19, 22t, Mogens Trolle 10, wildestanimal 12, Paul S Wolf 4-5c, 8.
t=top, r=right, l=left, c=centre, b=bottom
All artwork and other photography Brown Bear Books.

Every effort has been made to contact copyright holders of material reproduced in this book. Any omissions will be rectified in subsequent printings if notice is given to the publisher.

All the internet addresses (URLs) given in this book were valid at the time of going to press. However, due to the dynamic nature of the internet, some addresses may have changed, or sites may have changed or ceased to exist since publication. While the author and publisher regret any inconvenience this may cause readers, no responsibility for any such changes can be accepted by either the author or the publisher.

Contents

Meet the family 4

Animal Files
- Blue whale 6
- Humpback whale 8
- Grey whale 10
- Sperm whale 12
- Southern right whale 14
- Orca (killer whale) 16
- Bottlenose dolphin 18
- Narwhal 20

Quiz 22
Glossary 23
Find out more 24
Index 24

Meet the family

Whales and dolphins are mammals. They live in the oceans. But they come to the surface to breathe. Read on to find out more!

Sperm whale

Humpback whale

Bottlenose dolphin

Blue whale

Whales and Dolphins

Orca

Grey whale

Narwhal

Narwhals live in freezing Arctic seas. Polar bears and orcas hunt them.

Southern right whale

Blue whale

The blue whale is the biggest animal in the world. It is heavier than 40 elephants. Its heart weighs as much as a car!

FACT FILE

Scientific name: *Balaenoptera musculus*

Food: krill (tiny sea creatures), fish

Habitat: oceans all around the world

← tail

← blue grey skin

Whales breathe through a blowhole. They blow water through it too.

WHERE DOES IT LIVE?

Whales and Dolphins

small eye

blowhole for breathing

fin

grooves on throat and back

BIG OR SMALL

1.8 m (6 ft.)

24–30 m (80–100 ft.)

Blue whales "sing" to each other. The sounds are louder than an aeroplane. They travel hundreds of kilometres.

7

Humpback whale

Humpbacks are playful. They jump from the water! They twist their body as they leap. This is called breaching.

FACT FILE

Scientific name: *Megaptera novaeangliae*

Food: krill and small fish

Habitat: oceans all around the world; they live near the surface of the water

lumpy skin

This whale is breaching. It will make a big splash when it lands!

Grey whale

Grey whales feed on the seabed.
They dive to the bottom.
They suck their food from the mud.

FACT FILE

Scientific name: *Eschrichtius robustus*

Food: small invertebrates such as worms

Habitat: in the Pacific Ocean near the coast

tail

Grey whales have orange patches The patches are barnacles. They live on the whales' skin.

WHERE DOES IT LIVE?

Whales and Dolphins

grey skin

barnacles

paddle-shaped flipper

baby

BIG OR SMALL

1.8 m (6 ft.)

2–14 m (40–50 ft.)

Grey whales swim about 20,000 km (12,500 miles) each year. Over a lifetime, that's as far as to the Moon and back!

11

Sperm whale

This mighty whale hunts giant squid. It dives to the bottom of the ocean. It can hold its breath for up to two hours.

FACT FILE

Scientific name: *Physeter macrocephalus*

Food: squid, octopus, fish and cuttlefish

Habitat: all the world's oceans

massive, flat-ended head

Sperm whales live in groups called pods.

Whales and Dolphins

WHERE DOES IT LIVE?

- small hump
- tail
- wrinkled skin
- white patches on belly

BIG OR SMALL

1.8 m (6 ft.)

8–20 m (26–62 feet)

Sperm whales have the biggest brains of any animal. A car could fit inside a sperm whale's head!

13

Southern right whale

This whale is a slow swimmer.
It feeds on tiny sea creatures.
It catches them in its mouth as it swims.

FACT FILE

Scientific name:
Eubalaena australis

Food: tiny shrimp and plankton

Habitat: cold waters in the southern part of the world

wide tail

large flipper

The whale sticks its tail in the air. The wind pushes it along. This is called sailing.

WHERE DOES IT LIVE?

Whales and Dolphins

"bonnet" of lumpy skin

big head

BIG OR SMALL

1.8 m (6 ft.)

14–18 m (46–60 ft.)

The whales have lumps on their skin. The lumps have special names. There are eyebrows and bonnets!

15

Orca (killer whale)

Orcas are high-speed hunters.
They work as a team to catch prey.
Orcas will even attack sharks and whales.

FACT FILE

Scientific name: *Orcinus orca*

Food: fish, squid, seals, penguins, turtles, sharks, and even other whales

Habitat: open seas and coasts all around the world

rounded head

sharp teeth

Seals are an orca's favourite food. The whale will snatch one from a beach.

16

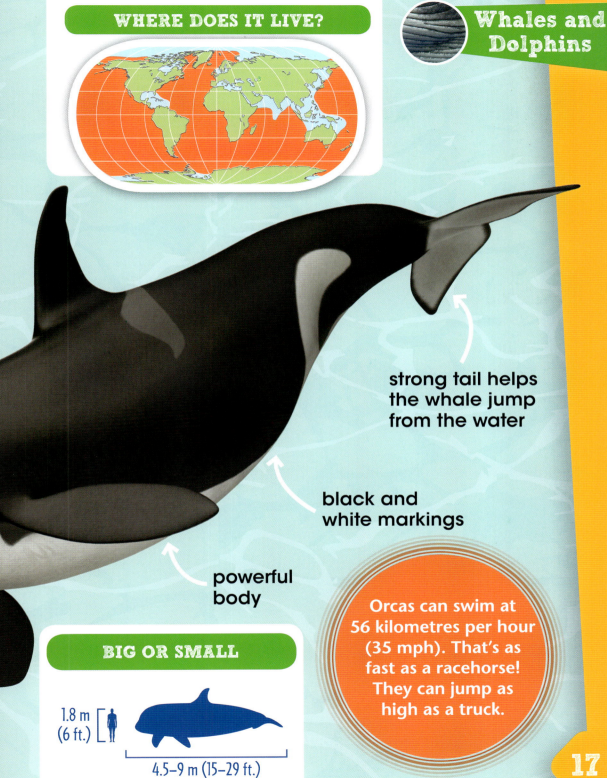

WHERE DOES IT LIVE?

Whales and Dolphins

strong tail helps the whale jump from the water

black and white markings

powerful body

BIG OR SMALL

1.8 m (6 ft.)

4.5–9 m (15–29 ft.)

Orcas can swim at 56 kilometres per hour (35 mph). That's as fast as a racehorse! They can jump as high as a truck.

17

Bottlenose dolphin

Dolphins are friendly and playful. They like to stroke their friends. They talk to each other with squeaks!

FACT FILE

Scientific name: *Tursiops truncatus*

Food: fish and squid

Habitat: cool and warm waters, often swim near the coast

pointed snout with sharp teeth

Dolphins love to play. These dolphins are jumping out of the water.

18

Narwhal

Narwhals are the unicorns of the sea. Male narwhals have an amazing tusk. It's a tooth that just keeps growing.

FACT FILE

Scientific name: *Monodon monoceros*

Food: fish, squid and shrimp

Habitat: coastal waters in oceans around the world

small head

Tusk

Narwhals swim in groups. Some groups just have females and their young. Other groups have males too.

WHERE DOES IT LIVE?

Whales and Dolphins

grey, brown spotted skin

lighter colour on belly

tail

short flipper

BIG OR SMALL

1.8 m (6 ft.)

4–5.5 m (13–18 ft.) not including the tusk

A narwhal's tusk can be 3 metres (10 feet) long. They are sometimes called "the unicorns of the sea".

Quiz

Test your skills! Can you answer these questions? Look in the book for clues. The answers are on page 24.

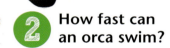

2 How fast can an orca swim?

1 Which whale catches fish with bubbles?

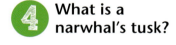

4 What is a narwhal's tusk?

3 What is the biggest animal in the world?

Glossary

Arctic
The far north of our planet. It is very cold all year round.

barnacle
A small sea creature with a shell.

fin
Body part that helps an animal swim.

habitat
The kind of place where an animal usually lives.

invertebrates
Animals that don't have a backbone.

pod
A group of whales or dolphins.

prey
An animal that is hunted by another animal for food.

Find out more

Books

Whales: An Illustrated Celebration, Kelsey Oseid (Ten Speed Press, 2018)

Whales and Dolphins (Eyewonder), DK (DK Children, 2013)

Websites

www.sciencekids.co.nz/sciencefacts/animals/dolphin.html

www.wdcs.org/wdcskids/en/index.php

Index

barnacles 10, 11
blowhole 6, 7
breaching 8

lumpy skin 9, 15

oceans 4, 6, 8, 12, 20

pods 12
polar bears 5
prey 16

seals 16
sharks 16
"singing" 7

teeth 16, 18
tusk 20, 21

Quiz answers: 1. The humpback whale. **2.** Up to 56 kilometres per hour (35 mph). **3.** The blue whale. **4.** A really long tooth.